A WONDERFUL WORLD OF WEATHER

Written by Kay Barnham

Illustrated by Maddie Frost

CRABTREE
PUBLISHING COMPANY
WWW.CRABTREEBOOKS.COM

CRABTREE
PUBLISHING COMPANY
WWW.CRABTREEBOOKS.COM

Author: Kay Barnham

Editorial Director: Kathy Middleton

Editors: Victoria Brooker, Janine Deschenes

Proofreader: Melissa Boyce

Creative director: Paul Cherrill

Illustrator: Maddie Frost

Production coordinator and
 Prepress technician: Tammy McGarr

Print coordinator: Katherine Berti

Words with lines underneath, like this, can be found in the glossary on page 32.

Library and Achives Canada Cataloguing in Publication

Title: A wonderful world of weather / written by Kay Barnham ; illustrated by
  Maddie Frost.
Names: Barnham, Kay, author. | Frost, Maddie, illustrator.
Description: Series statement: World of wonder | Originally published: London:
  Wayland, 2018. | Includes bibliographical references and index.
Identifiers: Canadiana (print) 20200220314 | Canadiana (ebook) 20200220322 |
  ISBN 9780778782469 (hardcover) |
  ISBN 9780778782506 (softcover) |
  ISBN 9781427126191 (HTML)
Subjects: LCSH: Weather—Juvenile literature. |
  LCSH: Meteorology—Juvenile literature.
Classification: LCC QC981.3 .B37 2021 | DDC j551.6—dc23

Library of Congress Cataloging-in-Publication Data

Names: Barnham, Kay, author. | Frost, Maddie, illustrator.
Title: A wonderful world of weather / written by Kay Barnham ;
  illustrated by Maddie Frost.
Description: New York : Crabtree Publishing Company, 2021. |
  Series: World of wonder | First published in 2018 by Wayland.
Identifiers: LCCN 2020015588 (print) | LCCN 2020015589 (ebook) |
  ISBN 9780778782469 (hardcover) | ISBN 9780778782506 (paperback) |
  ISBN 9781427126191 (ebook)
Subjects: LCSH: Weather--Juvenile literature.
Classification: LCC QC981.3 .B375 2021 (print) | LCC QC981.3 (ebook) |
  DDC 551.5--dc23
LC record available at https://lccn.loc.gov/2020015588
LC ebook record available at https://lccn.loc.gov/2020015589

Crabtree Publishing Company

www.crabtreebooks.com   1-800-387-7650
Published by Crabtree Publishing Company in 2021

First published in 2018 by Wayland
Copyright ©Hodder and Stoughton 2018

Printed in the U.S.A./072020/CG20200429

Published in Canada
Crabtree Publishing
616 Welland Avenue
St. Catharines, Ontario
L2M 5V6

Published in the United States
Crabtree Publishing
347 Fifth Ave
Suite 1402-145
New York, NY 10016

NOTES FOR PARENTS AND TEACHERS

This series encourages children to observe the wonderful world around them. Here are some ideas to help children get more out of this book.

1. Encourage children to keep a weather diary. Have them make observations about the weather they see each day. They can record their observations using words and pictures. Invite children to share their weather diaries with their peers.

2. Use homemade or real musical instruments to make weather noises. High notes on a piano might sound like tinkling rain. A drum made from a shoe box could sound like noisy thunder. Encourage children to be as imaginative as possible!

3. Make a rain gauge using an empty plastic water bottle. Cut the top off for children and then ask them to mark measurements up the side of the bottle. Then put the bottle outside and wait for a downpour! Have children write down the amount of rain collected. The next time you use the gauge, enourage children to predict how much rain they think might have fallen.

Did you know that there is a layer of <u>gases</u> around our planet? It is called the atmosphere. The atmosphere contains the air we breathe. It also protects us from the Sun's rays.

When sunlight warms the atmosphere, air swirls
around the world. This movement of air
makes all of our wonderful weather happen.

Today, the weather is sunny.
There are no clouds. The wind
is very light. The Sun shines
brightly in a clear, blue sky.

Sunny days can happen any time of
the year. They can happen in summer,
when the <u>temperature</u> is hot.
They can happen in winter,
when it might be snowy and cold.

Look at these fluffy clouds. They almost hide the Sun.
When the Sun is hidden, the temperature becomes cooler.

8

Clouds are made of tiny droplets of water and ice. First, the Sun warms bodies of water such as oceans and lakes. Water vapor rises from the warm water. As it rises, it cools and changes into the droplets that make up clouds.

9

Some clouds are dark and low
to the ground. Inside these
clouds, the water droplets
have grown bigger and heavier.

10

Splish, splash! Plip plop!

The water droplets are too heavy. They fall back to the ground as raindrops. It's time to open the umbrella!

When sunshine hits raindrops,
the Sun's light is split into different
colors. A rainbow of red, orange,
yellow, green, blue, indigo, and violet
light spreads across the sky.

Watch out for double
rainbows. These happen
when the sunlight is
<u>scattered</u> twice
by each raindrop!

13

When the temperature
is cold, ice crystals form
inside clouds. They stick
together to make snowflakes.
When they grow big and heavy,
the snowflakes begin to fall.

14

Every snowflake has six sides.
Each beautiful snowflake has a <u>unique</u> shape.

Sometimes, the temperature is too cold for rain and not cold enough for snow. Sleet is a <u>mixture</u> of rain and snow. It starts to melt as it falls to the ground.

Hailstones are lumps of ice
that form in some clouds.
Some hailstones are tiny.
Others are bigger
than ping pong balls!

Thunderclouds are
large and dark.
They sometimes look scary!
Rain, hail, thunder,
and lightning all come
from thunderclouds.

Lightning happens when
small pieces of ice inside
thunderclouds hit together.
Lightning flashes from cloud to
cloud and leaps down to the ground.
Thunder is the sound lightning makes.

Frost can appear when the temperature
drops below 32 °F (0 °C) at night.
At this temperature, water freezes.
Frost is frozen water vapor.

This spider's web is decorated with sparkly, twinkly frost.
Meanwhile, the puddle of water has frozen into ice.
Watch out! The ice is very slippery.

Mist happens when water vapor stays close to the ground.
A lot of mist can create a thick <u>fog</u>.

A thick fog makes it hard to see. People must travel very carefully. Cars travel slowly. Sometimes airplanes do not fly.

The Sun warms some parts of Earth's atmosphere more than others. When air is warm, it rises. At the same time, cool air sinks. Air is always moving. This movement causes wind.

Wind can be light and breezy. It can also
be very strong. Sometimes, wind blows
so hard that it is hard to walk against it!

Sometimes, weather can be dangerous. A hurricane is a huge storm. The wind is so strong that it can damage houses and blow down trees.

Hurricanes can also cause flooding. The strong winds can push ocean water onto the shore. Hurricanes can also bring a lot of rain.

27

A tornado is another dangerous storm.
It is a spinning column of air that sometimes
happens when there is a thunderstorm.
A tornado's wind is so strong that it
can pick up buildings, trees, and cars.

We can all take steps to stay safe from dangerous storms. We can watch weather <u>forecasts</u> that warn us about storms. We can <u>prepare</u> by gathering supplies or going to a safe place if we know a storm is coming.

THINGS TO DO

1. Everyone can be an artist! How many different types of weather can you fit into one painting? Look at the beautiful illustrations in this book for ideas.

2. Make a weather board game. Instead of Snakes and Ladders, you could play Sunshine and Showers! When a player lands on sunshine, move forward three spaces. When they land on showers, move back three spaces. Players roll dice to move their counters around the board.

3. Create a word cloud about the weather. Write "WEATHER" in the middle of the page. Then write all of the weather words you can think of. Write each word with a different-colored crayon or pencil. You could start like this:

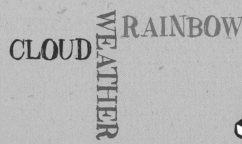

CLOUD WEATHER RAINBOW

LEARNING MORE

Books

Danks, Fiona, and Jo Schofield. *The Wild Weather Book*. Frances Lincoln, 2013.

Howell, Izzi. *Weather*. Wayland, 2016.

Johnson, Robin. *What Is Weather?* Crabtree Publishing, 2013.

Websites

Find more interesting weather facts at the NASA Climate Kids website. **www.climatekids.nasa.gov/menu/weather-and-climate/**

Learn more about weather forecasting and enjoy weather games, activities, jokes, and more. **www.weatherwizkids.com**

GLOSSARY

fog A cloud of tiny water droplets close to the ground

forecasts Predictions of future weather made by using tools and data, or information

gases Types of matter, such as air, that have no shape and expand freely

mixture Two or more substances mixed together

prepare To get ready for something before it happens

scattered Separated and went in many different directions

temperature A measure of how hot or cold something is

unique Unlike any other

water vapor Water that becomes a gas